GOD
STILL HEARS
AND
ANSWERS PRAYERS
REIGNITING FAITH & PASSION FOR PRAYING

PRAYER JOURNAL

DR. MARCIA LIVINGSTON-GALLOWAY

Fulton Books
Meadville, PA

Published by Fulton Books 2023

ISBN 979-8-88731-823-3 (paperback)
ISBN 979-8-88731-824-0 (digital)

Printed in the United States of America

I have written this to you who believe in the name of the Son of God, so that you may know you have eternal life. And we are confident that he hears us whenever we ask for anything that pleases him. And since we know he hears us when we make our requests, we also know that he will give us what we ask for.

—1 John 5:13-15 NLT

I will answer them before they even call to me. While they are still talking about their needs, I will go ahead and answer their prayers!

—Isaiah 65:24 NLT

Gifted to

Sadie

By

Kim

Date

1/28/24

GOD STILL HEARS AND ANSWERS THE
PRAYERS OF HIS CHILDREN. HE SAYS
YOU SHOULD CONTINUE TO PRAY AND
NOT GIVE UP! THANK YOU FOR PRAYING.

Dr. Marcia Livingston-Galloway.

Contents

Acknowledgements

This book is born out of the unwavering desire of the author to help practicing Christian believers worldwide to cultivate and embed the discipline of prayer in their Christian lives irrespective of where they are on their journey with Christ.

The COVID-19 pandemic created the time and opportunity to write and share daily prayers with family and friends all over the globe to encourage them to stay hopeful and faithful and to grow and mature in their faith in the midst of loss, despair, isolation, and fear.

I would not have compiled the prayers in this journal were it not for the encouragement and motivational support of several of the recipients of these prayers, particularly Deborah Tumey, and the professional and steady support of the Fulton publishing team, especially Charlyn Branca.

I wish to thank my supportive husband, Milton, for his encouragement, patience, and understanding during my many days and late nights writing.

Thanks to my RRTEC and Hope International Ministry families and friends across the globe who pray for me and gave their honest feedback on the artwork. Special thanks to Asia Thomas for painstakingly working on multiple reiterations of the cover design until the most fitting emerged, and to Ray Jackson for his skillful work of art included in this work.

Thank You, Lord, for Your inspiration!

A Note to the Prayer

Thank you for availing yourself of this resource. I am genuinely excited and joyfully expectant about the transformational impact that these prayers will have on you and those in your sphere of influence as you engage and partner with our heavenly Father to see His kingdom come and His will be done in our lives here on earth.

I wrote and compiled the prayers in this work during the height of the COVID-19 pandemic, which is still impacting the world at the time of this publication. God used these prayers to keep my faith anchored in Him when everything around seemed disheartening and hopeless. So it is with a deep sense of gratitude that I offer this work back to Him.

This journal is written to do the following:

1. Provide example prayers for new believers and for anyone who has decided to respond to God's prayer mandate regardless of where they are on their spiritual journey. God invites His children to partner with Him in establishing His kingdom on earth through ongoing prayers and intercessions for people in all nations (1 Timothy 2:1–4, 2 Chronicles 7:14, Luke 18:1).
2. Remind God's people that God has not and will never turn a deaf ear to our prayers. He is always listening and will exceed our expectations and imaginations (Jeremiah 33:3).
3. Assist believers who have become disenchanted with prayer to ignite or reignite their passion to pray so they may cultivate and experience deeper intimacy in their relationships with the Triune God who still hears and answers every prayer.

4. Yield to God. Give Him the *right of way* as we journey here on the earth so we might travel the road that leads to His expected end.

The journal can also be used to read and memorize God's Word. In addition to the scripture-based prayers, the journal also includes a space where you may record the dates you prayed these prayers and when you received your answers. There is also room for you to write your response to God or your own prayers. I invite you to share this resource and the testimonies of God's answers to your prayers.

Introduction

Prayer is one of the most ancient and significant practices among believers of all religions. Numerous books have been written on the subject, many dedicated to *how to pray*. During His life on earth, Jesus modeled a consistent, effective, and fruitful prayer life and emphasized its importance in the life of every believer. However, sadly enough, many in the Christian faith are neither committed to a life of prayer nor do they seem convinced of its efficacy. Many debate the necessity of prayer because to them, it appears as if God does whatever He wants and gives to who He wants whether they pray to Him or not. You may be one of those individuals. If you are, you are not alone. I have had many moments when I have questioned whether or not my prayers are being heard. So why do I continue to pray? I continue because as I set out to study God's Word on the topic of prayer, I have discovered three fundamental truths about prayer that we have not always been taught in church:

(1) God always hears and answers our prayers in one of three ways: yes, no, or wait (Psalm 40:1; 2 Samuel 5:19, 23; 2 Samuel 12:15–18; 1 Kings 8:18–19; John 11:5–6, 17). God's prayer promises are conditional. There are often ifs and ands that you and I need to meet for answered prayers (2 Chronicles 7:14, John 15:7).

(2) Prayer requires faith in God (Hebrews 11:6) and a knowledge of His will (1 John 5: 14–15).

(3) Prayer is a *means* whereby humans commune and partner with God to advance His kingdom purpose and will in our lives and the affairs of the earth (Matthew 6:10, Jeremiah

29:12, Romans 10:1) and listen for His responses (during and after).

Jesus taught that good parents would not give their children a stone or serpent if they asked for bread or fish. Neither would they give their children a stone or serpent even if they asked for it. Why? Because good parents respond to their children with wisdom and love. How much more our heavenly Father? He would never give us anything that is harmful even if we repeatedly ask for it. God gives only good gifts to His children (Matthew 7:11, Psalm 84:11).

Inputs and Outcomes

The outcome of any process is usually contingent on its inputs. In the same way oxygen is the critical input for humans to live and the addition of yeast to the ingredients for a loaf of bread to rise, there are some essential elements that must be present for God to hear and answer our prayers. Among these elements are faith, trust, admission and confession of our sins, worship, and thanksgiving. God says He will not hear us if we have sin and unforgiveness in our hearts (Psalm 66:18). Besides, He requires faith in Him and a sincere heart (Hebrews 11:6).

The COVID-19 pandemic has created havoc in nations and produced death, destruction, separation, isolation, fear, mistrust, anxiety, hopelessness, disunity, and confusion—all negative inputs for effective prayer outcomes. What does one do in times like these? Pray! God invites us to pray when we are in trouble, although that should not be the only time (James 5:13–16). Unfortunately, many who turned to God for help in prayer and did not receive the answers they expected either hate God for it, walk away with the belief that God does not hear or care, or question whether He still hears and answers prayers. The truth is many practicing Christian believers also ask many of the same questions. Yet despite our questions, we have learned that God answers our prayers in the midst of challenges and storms and uses them as opportunities for us to strengthen and grow our faith and to live what we profess. Yes, God understands our emotions, but He wants us to respond to our storms by trusting and drawing nearer to Him. If you are undecided about trusting Christ for salvation, I encourage you not to delay accepting this free gift. Know that God has not abandoned you and that He wants to have a personal relationship with you.

John Stott notes that God denies our prayer requests if the things we ask for are "either not good in themselves, or not good for us or for others, directly or indirectly, immediately or ultimately." Therefore, do not give up praying. Through prayer, God partners with His church to establish His will in their lives and on the earth. As St. Augustine notes, "Without God, man cannot, and without man, God will not [*do what He assigned us to do*]." Thus, it is important for all of God's children to engage in praying (1 Thessalonians 5:17).

Jesus's disciples noticed that when He prayed, His prayers produced results. When they asked Him to teach them how to pray, He gave them *the template* that we call the *Lord's Prayer*. As Jesus's disciples, we can also use the same template when we bring our petitions or cases to Him. However, it is important that we fill in the template with the portions of God's Word that are relevant to our specific cases. In case you are wondering, why? The answer is not complicated. It is simply because God's Word is the constitution of heaven, and it contains all the rights and privileges of every believer.

It is essential that we know the rights that God says we have if we are citizens in His kingdom. These rights outlined in heaven's constitution cannot be reversed by any person or legislative body on earth! Therefore, it is very important that we know what they are by reading, memorizing, studying, and meditating on God's Word. Remember also that God is the Righteous Judge (Deuteronomy 32:36, Psalm 19:9), and He will adjudicate fairly on behalf of all those who seek His advocacy. He will never allow the enemy to triumph over His precious children!

Know that as sons of God (John 1:12), we have a right to come to God with our prayers and petitions because Jesus Christ gave us access by shedding His blood as a payment for our sin that separated us from God the Father. Consequently, Jesus's blood has become the access code to God's throne room. All who enter into a right relationship with Jesus Christ have been given this code and have full and free access into the presence of our heavenly Father (Ephesians 2:18). There we can commune with Him and bring our requests to Him.

God still hears and answers prayers. He told the Israelites He would answer their prayers before they even called on Him, and while they are still telling Him about their needs, He would go ahead and answer their prayers (Isaiah 65:24). God's ears are not heavy, and His hand is not short (Isaiah 59:1–2). In fact, He invites us to bring our requests to Him. (Jeremiah 33:3, Matthew 7: 7–8, Philippians 4:6). Please understand and remember that God is sovereign. So as Dr. Myles Munroe once stated, God may not give us an explanation for everything He does or for how He chooses to answer our prayers, but He will definitely reveal Himself to us. Furthermore, lest we start taking credit, it is very important to understand that there are countless things that God has done and will do for our benefit that we have never or will ever pray about.

If you have not yet accepted Jesus Christ's offer of salvation and started your relationship with Him, I invite you to do so now so you, too, can fully experience answered prayers. Your first answered prayer occurs the moment you acknowledge your need of Him, repent of your sins, and invite Him into your life (John 9: 31, 1 John 1:9). What challenges and storms are you facing right now? I invite you to take them to God in prayer. Anchor your trust in Him. He listens well, and He still hears and answers prayers.

Be sure to document the date(s) when you prayed each prayer and track your answers on the lines at the bottom of each page. With that said, let us pray!

Personal Anchors
Foundational Prayers

Accepting Salvation by Faith in Christ

For this is how God loved the world: He gave his one and only Son, so that everyone who believes in him will not perish but have eternal life.

—John 3: 16 NLT

🙏 Prayer 🙏

Dear God, my Father, my heart is filled with gratitude because You sacrificed Your only Son so I can spend eternity with You. I bow my heart in humble adoration and reverent awe of You. You are the reason I am alive, and I am forever grateful for Your breath in my lungs and joy in my heart. I choose to live and believe in You. Thank You for Your eternal life! In Christ Jesus's name. Amen.

Intercession

Pray for those yet to come into the right relationship with Christ (your family and others here and abroad) that they may personally experience Christ's salvation. 🕊 🕊 🕊

Dates:

Prayed _____ Answered _____

Personal Notes

_____

_____

_____

_____

_____

_____

_____

_____

_____

_____

_____

_____

_____

_____

Pleasing God

And it is impossible to please God without
faith. Anyone who wants to come to him
must believe that God exists and that he
rewards those who sincerely seek him.

—Hebrews 11:6 NLT

🙏 Prayer 🙏

Father God, today I am thankful that I can come to You in faith. I admit my faith still wavers sometimes, but in a way I cannot explain, deep down I believe You exist for real and You answer the prayers of those who call upon You in honesty and sincerity. I place myself in your hands and leave the rest up to You. In Christ Jesus's name. Amen.

Intercession

Pray for others who believe that there is a God but still have some doubt that they would put their faith in Christ Jesus no matter how small it is. 🕊️ 🕊️ 🕊️

Dates:

Prayed _____ Answered _____

Personal Notes

_____

_____

_____

_____

_____

_____

_____

_____

_____

_____

_____

_____

_____

_____

Dr. Marcia Livingston-Galloway

Becoming a Child of God

But to all who believed him and accepted him,
he gave the right to become children of God.

—John 1:12 NLT

🙏 Prayer 🙏

Loving Lord and Father, thank You for exposing me to Your word and helping me to understand how easy it is to become Your child. I accept You as my Lord and Savior. Thank You for adopting me into Your family and giving me access to everything You have in Your kingdom. Help me from this day forward to live a life that shows I belong to You. In Christ Jesus's name. Amen.

Intercession

Pray for those who are still blinded by sin that God would open their eyes to salvation. 🕊 🕊 🕊

Dates:

Prayed _____ Answered _____

Personal Notes

_____

_____

_____

_____

_____

_____

_____

_____

_____

_____

_____

_____

_____

_____

_____

Freedom from Condemnation

So now there is no condemnation for
those who belong to Christ Jesus.

—Romans 8:1 NLT

🙏 Prayer 🙏

Father God, hallowed be Your name. Thank You that I can come to You just as I am. Sometimes I feel downtrodden and discouraged because of the mistakes I've made. But I'm encouraged by Your word, which reminds me that You never condemn anyone who has put their faith in Christ Jesus. Thank You for your forgiveness and restoration. In Christ Jesus's name. Amen.

Intercession

Pray for people who are living under condemnation and guilt that they would forgive themselves and embrace the forgiveness of Christ. 🕊 🕊 🕊

Dates:

Prayed _____ Answered _____

Personal Notes

_____

_____

_____

_____

_____

_____

_____

_____

_____

_____

_____

_____

_____

_____

Developing a Submissive Heart

And I will give you a new heart, and I
will put a new spirit in you. I will take
out your stony, stubborn heart, and
give you a tender, responsive heart.

—Ezekiel 36:26 NLT

🙏 Prayer 🙏

Holy Father and Lord, I come to You today in the name of Jesus Christ who gave His life so I can have eternal life. Thank You for this gift! I humbly ask You to give me a heart like Yours—a heart of compassion and love, one that is responsive, obedient, unselfish, and moldable in Your hands. Father, I want to be like You in everything I say and do. In Christ Jesus's name. Amen.

Intercession

Pray for people with stubborn, unbelieving hearts that God would soften their hearts to hear and respond to the gospel of Jesus Christ. 🕊️ 🕊️ 🕊️

Dates:

Prayed _____ Answered _____

Personal Notes

_____

_____

_____

_____

_____

_____

_____

_____

_____

_____

_____

_____

_____

_____

_____

Combating Fear and Discouragement

Don't be afraid, for I am with you. Don't
be discouraged, for I am your God. I will
strengthen you and help you. I will hold
you up with My victorious right hand.

—Isaiah 41:10 NLT

🙏 Prayer 🙏

Jehovah God, thank You for another day. I love and appreciate You for always giving me the word of encouragement I need at the right time. Father, I feel overwhelmed, but I trust in You. When I am fearful, remind me that Your perfect love casts out fear. Let the knowledge of who You are and the truths in Your word sink deep in my soul and my spirit and change the way I think today. Father, no matter what I face any given day, help me to remember that You are my present help and that you will strengthen me. In Christ Jesus's name. Amen.

Intercession

Pray for those who live alone, especially those who have lost or disconnected from their loved ones. 🕊 🕊 🕊

Dates:

Prayed _____ Answered _____

Personal Notes

_____

_____

_____

_____

_____

_____

_____

_____

_____

_____

_____

_____

_____

_____

_____

To Be Truly Free

So Christ has truly set us free. Now make
sure that you stay free, and don't get
tied up again in slavery to the law.

—Galatians 5:1 NLT

🙏 Prayer 🙏

Holy Father and Lord, thank You for who You are and for all
You are doing in me. I'm grateful to You, Christ Jesus, for setting me
free from the bondage of sin through Your death, burial, and resur-
rection. Your sacrifice sets me free from my mistakes and sinful past
and is enough. Help me to choose freedom every moment of the day
by choosing to obey Your word and not giving in to the desires of my
flesh. I pray my life will be an authentic representation of freedom in
Christ. In Christ Jesus's name. Amen.

Intercession

Pray for those who have been delivered from drugs, alcohol, and
other addictions that they will avoid people, situations, and activities
that will lure them back into those habits. 🕊 🕊 🕊

Dates:

Prayed _____ Answered _____

Personal Notes

_____

_____

_____

_____

_____

_____

_____

_____

_____

_____

_____

_____

_____

_____

_____

_____

To Stay Pure

Purify me from my sins, and I will be clean;
wash me, and I will be whiter than snow.

—Psalm 51:7 NLT

🙏 Prayer 🙏

Loving and forgiving Father, I come to You humbly in the name of Christ Jesus. I confess I have been trying to get my life right before coming to You, but I have been unsuccessful. I know You know my heart, and I need You to help me to change. I am sorry for sinning against You and for intentionally hurting myself and others. I admit I am addicted to sin and need Your deliverance! I want every part of my life to glorify You. Cleanse me thoroughly of all my sins; purify my mind and heart so there will be permanent change in the way I live. Make me new, I pray. Thank You, Father. In Christ Jesus's name. Amen.

Intercession

Pray for believers who are secretly struggling with habitual sins.

🕊️ 🕊️ 🕊️

Dates:

Prayed _____ Answered _____

Personal Notes

_____

_____

_____

_____

_____

_____

_____

_____

_____

_____

_____

_____

_____

_____

_____

Putting My Hope in God's Word

I am counting on the Lord; yes, I am counting
on him. I have put my hope in his word.

—Psalm 130:5 NLT

🙏 Prayer 🙏

Father God, thank You for another earth day and the precious gift of life. I have no idea what today brings, so I'm counting on You to lead, guide, and direct my thoughts and steps. Help me to look and listen attentively for Your instructions and follow Your lead. Help me not to allow impatience to get the better of me. I place my hope and confident trust in You, knowing You will not disappoint me. In Christ Jesus's name. Amen.

Intercession

Pray earnestly for people who have lost or are losing confidence in God's word because of various disappointments in life. 🕊 🕊 🕊

Dates:

Prayed _____ Answered _____

Personal Notes

_____

_____

_____

_____

_____

_____

_____

_____

_____

_____

_____

_____

_____

_____

_____

_____

Trusting and
Depending on God

Trust in the Lord with all your heart; do
not depend on your own understanding.
Seek his will in all you do, and he will
show you which path to take.

—Proverbs 3:5–6 NLT

🙏 Prayer 🙏

Heavenly Father and Lord, I come to You today with a thankful heart. I'm extremely grateful to You for guiding me even those times when I was not aware. I am glad I don't have to navigate life on my own. I give You full control of the wheels of my life and ask for Your leading throughout this day. I trust that no matter what, I will be safe and successful because You will direct my steps. In Christ Jesus's name. Amen.

Intercession

Pray for family, friends, and others who need God's direction today, especially those having to make tough decisions. 🕊 🕊 🕊

Dates:

Prayed _____ Answered _____

Personal Notes

_____

_____

_____

_____

_____

_____

_____

_____

_____

_____

_____

_____

_____

_____

Finding Comfort in Times of Doubt

When doubts filled my mind, your comfort
gave me renewed hope and cheer.

—Psalm 94:19 NLT

🙏 Prayer 🙏

Our gracious God and heavenly Father, thank You for Jesus Christ who gives me confidence and assurance when I am filled with doubt. As I face life-changing decisions (marriage, interviews, court, divorce, death, etc.), today help me to remember that I do not face them alone, for You are with me. I am grateful I can trust You with all my anxious thoughts. Thank You for the joy, renewed hope, and comfort I have in You. In Christ Jesus's name. Amen.

Intercession

Pray for those who are facing a life-changing situation today. Ask God to give them the hope and confidence they need. 🕊 🕊 🕊

Dates:

Prayed _____ Answered _____

Personal Notes

_____

_____

_____

_____

_____

_____

_____

_____

_____

_____

_____

_____

_____

_____

_____

_____

Engaging in Continual Praise

I will praise the Lord at all times. I will
constantly speak his praises. I will boast only
in the Lord; let all who are helpless take heart.

—Psalm 34:1–2 NLT

🙏 Prayer 🙏

Holy Father and Lord, thank You for a brand-new day and for all the blessings that come with it. I will bless Your name every chance I get. No matter what happens, with the help of the Holy Spirit, I will give You thanks, praise, and worship because You are worthy. You inhabit the praises of Your people, so I will build a home for You with my praises. I will boast about You and give the credit for all my successes to You alone! In Christ Jesus's name, I pray. Amen.

Intercession

Pray for your family and friends who constantly gripe and complain about everything that they would identify at least one thing to praise God for every day. 🕊 🕊 🕊

Dates:

Prayed _____ Answered _____

Personal Notes

_____

_____

_____

_____

_____

_____

_____

_____

_____

_____

_____

_____

_____

_____

_____

The Inner Life Transformational Prayers

Living as a New Creation

This means that anyone who belongs to
Christ has become a new person. The
old life is gone; a new life has begun!

—2 Corinthians 5:17 NLT

🙏 Prayer 🙏

Dear Father God, it is amazing how You are transforming my life from the moment I confessed my sins and accepted Your gift of salvation. Thank You! I understand I need to show that I have changed my allegiance from the devil and his kingdom to Yours. Please help me to live as Jesus Christ did. Holy Spirit, please guide and correct me, teach me to do what is right, and hold me accountable. In Christ Jesus's name. Amen.

Intercession

Pray for believers everywhere that how we live will be consistent with what we profess and that we bring honor to the Lord's name.
🕊 🕊 🕊

Dates:

Prayed _____ Answered _____

Personal Notes

_____

_____

_____

_____

_____

_____

_____

_____

_____

_____

_____

_____

_____

_____

Remedy for Sin

I have hidden your word in my heart,
that I might not sin against you.

—Psalm 119:11 NLT

🙏 Prayer 🙏

Patient Father and loving God, my heart is filled with gratitude that You did not and will never let me stay in my sins. You have given me the remedy for my sin problem in Your written and spoken word. Give me a deeper hunger and appetite for Your word so I will grow and mature as a believer. Help me to read, memorize, and meditate on Your word so I do not sin against you and others. Today I choose to meditate on Your word. In Christ Jesus's name. Amen.

Intercession

Pray that God will give every believer an appetite for His word.

🕊 🕊 🕊

Dates:

Prayed _____ Answered _____

Personal Notes

_____

_____

_____

_____

_____

_____

_____

_____

_____

_____

_____

_____

_____

_____

_____

_____

Dr. Marcia Livingston-Galloway

Worshipping God with All My Heart

Let all that I am praise the LORD; with my whole heart, I will praise his holy name. Let all that I am praise the LORD; may I never forget the good things he does for me.

—Psalm 103:1–2 NLT

🙏 Prayer 🙏

Father God, I come to You with a heart full of gratitude. Thanks for the creative mind and the strength and abilities You have given to me to accomplish every task today. I am grateful for the creative ideas and help You give me on difficult tasks and in difficult situations. Thank You for all my loved ones. Thank You for every provision. Thank You for health and healing. Thank You for keeping me and for being present with me always. Lord, thanks for the collaborative work of the Godhead for my overall well-being. I love You, and I am grateful that You are in my life. In Christ Jesus's name. Amen.

Intercession

Pray that believers everywhere would remember God's goodness and worship Him with all their hearts and souls. 🕊️ 🕊️ 🕊️

Dates:

Prayed _____ Answered _____

Personal Notes

_____

_____

_____

_____

_____

_____

_____

_____

_____

_____

_____

_____

_____

_____

_____

Living Honestly and Wisely

But you desire honesty from the womb,
teaching me wisdom even there.

—Psalm 51:6 NLT

🙏 Prayer 🙏

Dear heavenly Father, I am very glad You are in my life. I am grateful for the example of Jesus Christ who lived a life that did not compromise Your truth. I desire to live a life of honesty and integrity no matter the consequences. Teach me wisdom from Your word, and help me to practice what I learn. Remind me that what is inside of me is what will come out in my speech and my lifestyle. I pray my life will be marked by the virtues of Christ and will attract others to You. In Christ Jesus's name. Amen.

Intercession

Pray for those who are raising children and overseeing youth ministries that God will help them to teach and practice honesty and integrity. 🕊️ 🕊️ 🕊️

Dates:

Prayed _____ Answered _____

Personal Notes

_____

_____

_____

_____

_____

_____

_____

_____

_____

_____

_____

_____

_____

_____

_____

_____

Managing Earthly Treasures

Don't store up treasures here on earth,
where moths eat them and rust destroys
them, and where thieves break in and
steal. Store your treasures in heaven,
where moths and rust cannot destroy,
and thieves do not break in and steal.

—Matthew 6:19–20 NLT

🙏 Prayer 🙏

Eternal God and Father, I thank You for every resource You have given to me. I realize that everything I have belongs to You. I did not bring anything into the world with me and will leave everything here. Help me to be generous with all the things You have blessed me with (name some specifically). Teach me to give discerningly and joyfully, especially to those who are poor and destitute, and to those in the body of Christ. Thank You for being my source. In Christ Jesus's name. Amen.

Intercession

Pray for those with surplus (food, clothing, money, etc.) that they would willingly share what they have with those who have nothing instead of keeping it for themselves. 🕊 🕊 🕊

Dates:

Prayed _____ Answered _____

Personal Notes

_____

_____

_____

_____

_____

_____

_____

_____

_____

_____

_____

_____

_____

_____

Loving Others Sincerely

You were cleansed from your sins when you
obeyed the truth, so now you must show
sincere love to each other as brothers and sisters.
Love each other deeply with all your heart.

—1 Peter 1:22 NLT

🙏 Prayer 🙏

Great God and eternal Father, I pause this minute to say thank You for all You are and for what You are doing in me. Your word commands me to love others with all my heart, yet sometimes I find it difficult to do so, especially loving those who have wronged me, my family, and my friends. You love me in spite of all my mess so I can love others also. Thank You for loving all of us even when we don't deserve it. So today I choose to love Your creation by the help of the Holy Spirit. I desire to be more like Jesus Christ. Help me, I pray. In Christ Jesus's name. Amen.

Intercession

Pray for those who do not love themselves and have a tough time receiving love. 🕊️ 🕊️ 🕊️

Dates:

Prayed_____ Answered_____

Personal Notes

_____

_____

_____

_____

_____

_____

_____

_____

_____

_____

_____

_____

_____

_____

_____

Dr. Marcia Livingston-Galloway

Remaining Joyful

Always be full of joy in the Lord.
I say it again—rejoice!

—Philippians 4:4 NLT

🙏 Prayer 🙏

Gracious heavenly Father, I come to You this day with a sad heart when I think of the challenges in my life and the lives of family, friends, and humans as a whole. Thank You that I can find joy in Your presence and for giving me a garment of praise for the spirit of heaviness. I praise you for hope, strength, courage, and fortitude in the midst of troubled times. I declare I have the joy of the Lord because of Jesus Christ. Regardless of my situation, help me to remain joyful. In Christ Jesus's name. Amen.

Intercession

Pray for Christians who are imprisoned, persecuted, or ostracized because of their allegiance to Christ that the joy of the Lord would be their strength and for their safety and eventual freedom! 🕊️ 🕊️ 🕊️

Dates:

Prayed _____ Answered _____

Personal Notes

_____

_____

_____

_____

_____

_____

_____

_____

_____

_____

_____

_____

_____

_____

_____

_____

Cultivating a Godly Thought Life

And now, dear brothers and sisters, one final
thing. Fix your thoughts on what is true,
and honorable, and right, and pure, and
lovely, and admirable. Think about things
that are excellent and worthy of praise.

—Philippians 4:8 NLT

🙏 Prayer 🙏

Our Father in heaven, I honor and revere Your name. Thank You
for showing me how to live as a child of God. Father, my mind is a
constant battlefield where all kinds of thoughts are trying to control
my decisions and choices. There is always a battle in my mind when I
am praying or reading Your Word. Please help me to focus my mind on
things that are pure, honest, virtuous, noteworthy, true, and praisewor-
thy rather than on what is negative and unwholesome. I declare I have
victory with the help of the Holy Spirit. In Christ Jesus's name. Amen.

Intercession

Pray for people who tend to dwell on negative thoughts and for
those holding grudges against others. 🕊 🕊 🕊

Dates:

Prayed _____ Answered _____

Personal Notes

_____

_____

_____

_____

_____

_____

_____

_____

_____

_____

_____

_____

_____

_____

_____

Praying with the Right Motives

You want what you don't have, so you scheme
and kill to get it. You are jealous of what others
have, but you can't get it, so you fight and wage
war to take it away from them. Yet you don't
have what you want because you don't ask
God for it. And even when you ask, you don't
get it because your motives are all wrong—
you want only what will give you pleasure.

—James 4:2–3 NLT

🙏 Prayer 🙏

Great God and Father, thank You for the privilege of a new day and for allowing me to have honest conversations with You. I confess that sometimes I come to You and do not know what to ask for. Other times I pray with selfish motives or I am jealous of those whose prayers are answered. Please forgive me. Help me to put away arrogance and pride and to put on honesty, sincerity, and humility. Help me also to rejoice with those who receive answers to their prayers. Thank You, Father. In Christ Jesus's name. Amen.

Intercession

Pray for those who are motivated by greed or have committed themselves to doing wrong to get things they do not need. Ask God to reveal His will to them. 🕊 🕊 🕊

Dates:

Prayed _____ Answered _____

Personal Notes

_____

_____

_____

_____

_____

_____

_____

_____

_____

_____

_____

Knowing God's Ways and Thoughts

"My thoughts are nothing like your thoughts,"
says the Lord. "And my ways are far beyond
anything you could imagine. For just as
the heavens are higher than the earth, so
my ways are higher than your ways and my
thoughts higher than your thoughts."

—Isaiah 55:8–9 NLT

🙏 Prayer 🙏

Almighty God and Father, how majestic is Your name, and how vast Your wisdom! You are the all-knowing God. There is absolutely nothing that can be hidden from You, yet You do not force Yourself on us. Please show me how to align my heart and ways with Your heart and my thoughts with Your thoughts so whatever I think, say, and do might be agreeable with You. In Christ Jesus's name. Amen.

Intercession

Pray for God's wisdom and intervention in decision-making for church and political leaders, college graduates, medical practitioners, and business operators. 🕊 🕊 🕊

Dates:

Prayed _____ Answered _____

Personal Notes

_____

_____

_____

_____

_____

_____

_____

_____

_____

_____

_____

_____

_____

_____

_____

_____

Following God's Plan

"For I know the plans I have for you," says the Lord. "They are plans for good and not for disaster, to give you a future and a hope. In those days when you pray, I will listen. If you look for me wholeheartedly, you will find me."

—Jeremiah 29:11–13 NLT

🙏 Prayer 🙏

Glorious Lord and Father, thank You for working all things out for my good and the good of those in my sphere of influence. I am grateful that You have a plan for my life. I am confident that Your plan is better than mine, so please help me to check in with You regularly to ensure I remain in Your plan. I love and appreciate You for who You are and ask that Your plans will prevail in my life. In Christ Jesus's name. Amen.

Intercession

Pray for national and international leaders that they will seek God's plan and allow him to override the ones that are not beneficial to those they lead. 🕊️ 🕊️ 🕊️

Dates:

Prayed _____ Answered _____

Personal Notes

_____

_____

_____

_____

_____

_____

_____

_____

_____

_____

_____

_____

_____

_____

_____

Dr. Marcia Livingston-Galloway

Staying Connected to God

Remain in me, and I will remain in you.
For a branch cannot produce fruit if it is
severed from the vine, and you cannot
be fruitful unless you remain in me.

—John 15:4 NLT

🙏 Prayer 🙏

Gracious God and eternal Savior, I am thankful for You and
for abundant life. I know several hours have passed since I awoke,
and I'm now just having a quiet moment to worship and hear You!
Father, I want my life to be fruitful and for others to benefit from
the fruits of my life. Therefore, I commit to staying connected to
You as You are my life source. Apart from You, I'm as good as dead. I
give everything to You that is not good or beneficial for my spiritual
growth and my effectiveness here on earth. In Christ Jesus's name.
Amen.

Intercession

Pray for believers who have disconnected from their faith and
isolated themselves from other believers. 🕊 🕊 🕊

Dates:

Prayed _____ Answered _____

Personal Notes

_____

_____

_____

_____

_____

_____

_____

_____

_____

_____

_____

_____

_____

_____

_____

Developing a Spirit-Controlled Mind

So letting your sinful nature control your mind leads to death. But letting the Spirit control your mind leads to life and peace.

—Romans 8:6 NLT

🙏 Prayer 🙏

Father God, thank You for always having me on Your mind. I confess I struggle to focus on You even during my devotional time. I've often allowed things that don't matter to consume my thoughts. Please forgive me, and help me to change the way I think. By the help of the Holy Spirit, help me to fill my mind with Your word and with thoughts that please You so I may experience Your peace. In Christ Jesus's name. Amen.

Intercession

Pray for other believers who are increasingly distracted by their thoughts and social media that God would give them a disciplined mind. 🕊️ 🕊️ 🕊️

Dates:

Prayed _____ Answered _____

Personal Notes

_____

_____

_____

_____

_____

_____

_____

_____

_____

_____

_____

_____

_____

_____

Guarding My Mouth

Those who control their tongue will have a long
life; opening your mouth can ruin everything.

—Proverbs 13:3 NLT

🙏 Prayer 🙏

Our Father God, we give praise and honor to Your glorious
name. Lord, we know You do not waste words or use words thought-
lessly. Your words are powerful and life-giving. Lord, we confess we
have a problem with our mouths. We don't always say things that
are pleasant or helpful to others or ourselves. We can be mean and
unkind with our words, so we are asking for Your help. Take control
of what we say, Lord, and guard our lips. Forgive us for the times
we disgraced Your name. Teach us to speak encouragement, peace,
and life, especially when we are tempted to do otherwise. Help us to
cooperate with the Holy Spirit when He tells us to be quiet or how
to speak truth with grace. We ask these things in Christ Jesus's name.
Amen.

Intercession

Pray for other believers who struggle with knowing when to
speak and when to be quiet. 🕊 🕊 🕊

Dates:

Prayed _____ Answered _____

Personal Notes

_____

_____

_____

_____

_____

_____

_____

_____

_____

_____

_____

_____

_____

_____

Dr. Marcia Livingston-Galloway

Practicing True Worship

And so, dear brothers and sisters, I plead with
you to give your bodies to God because of all
he has done for you. Let them be a living and
holy sacrifice—the kind he will find acceptable.
This is truly the way to worship him.

—Romans 12:1 NLT

🙏 Prayer 🙏

Holy Father God, thank You for Your mercies that are new every day. In response to Your love, mercy, and grace I want my entire life to glorify You. Forgive me for misrepresenting You in the inconsistent way I have been living. I realize I do not fully understand what it means to be the living sacrifice You desire. I willingly make sacrifices for people sometimes without counting the cost but find that I am not as willing to make sacrifices for kingdom work. Teach me how to live faithful and holy. I give You all of me today. In Christ Jesus's name. Amen.

Intercession

Pray for those who struggle to live a committed and holy Christian life. 🕊️ 🕊️ 🕊️

Dates:

Prayed _____ Answered _____

Personal Notes

_____

_____

_____

_____

_____

_____

_____

_____

_____

_____

_____

_____

_____

_____

Resisting Temptations

The temptations in your life are no
different from what others experience.
And God is faithful. He will not allow
the temptation to be more than you can
stand. When you are tempted, he will show
you a way out so that you can endure.

—1 Corinthians 10:13 NLT

🙏 Prayer 🙏

My heavenly Father who lives in heaven and my heart, holy is Your name. May Your instructions in Your Word guide my every thought and deed. Lead me not into temptation, Lord. I know the enemy stays busy trying to make me sin by disobeying You. Help me to recognize him immediately, and by the power of Your Spirit, show me how to escape him. Where I am weak, give me the strength to resist him, Father. Thank You for leading me to Your divine will. In Christ Jesus's name. Amen.

Intercession

Pray for others you know who are struggling to resist the temptations that they consistently yield to. 🕊️ 🕊️ 🕊️

Dates:

Prayed _____ Answered _____

Personal Notes

_____

_____

_____

_____

_____

_____

_____

_____

_____

_____

_____

_____

_____

_____

_____

_____

Living a Prosperous and Successful Life

Study this Book of Instruction continually.
Meditate on it day and night so you will be
sure to obey everything written in it. Only then
will you prosper and succeed in all you do.

—Joshua 1:8 NLT

🙏 Prayer 🙏

Dear heavenly Father, You are the wise, all-knowing God. Nothing is hidden from You. I acknowledge that my understanding and my views are limited. Regardless of my education or what I already know, You said if I study Your word consistently and meditate on it all day and obey it, I will be prosperous and successful. Guide me in my study of Your word and help me to understand success from Your perspective. As I study, please show me the specific plans you have for me each day. Thank You for good success. In Christ Jesus's name. Amen.

Intercession

Pray for those in leadership that they will seek God's counsel as they contemplate and make decisions that will impact the lives of many. 🕊️ 🕊️ 🕊️

Dates:

Prayed _____ Answered _____

Personal Notes

_____

_____

_____

_____

_____

_____

_____

_____

_____

_____

_____

_____

_____

_____

_____

_____

Achieving the Peace of God

Keep putting into practice all you learned
and received from me—everything you
heard from me and saw me doing. Then
the God of peace will be with you.

—Philippians 4:9 NLT

🙏 Prayer 🙏

Eternal God and everlasting Father, thank You for the perfect example of Jesus Christ, Your Son, and for Your written word that also gives us examples of people who lived a committed Christian life. Help me to commit to putting the lessons You reveal in Your word into practice today. Please make my thoughts agreeable with Your thoughts and align my heart with Yours. I give You complete access to every area of my life. I am ready to obey and live by the principles in Your word. In Christ Jesus's name. Amen.

Intercession

Pray for all believers everywhere who live half-hearted Christian lives and are willing to obey only some of what God teaches in His Word. 🕊️ 🕊️ 🕊️

Dates:

Prayed _____ Answered _____

Personal Notes

_____

_____

_____

_____

_____

_____

_____

_____

_____

_____

_____

_____

_____

_____

_____

_____

Undivided Loyalty

Come close to God, and God will come
close to you. Wash your hands, you sinners;
purify your hearts, for your loyalty is
divided between God and the world.

—James 4:8 NLT

🙏 Prayer 🙏

Father God, thank You for allowing me to spend time with You whenever I want to. I honestly admit I do not make You a priority or spend time with You like I want to. Instead, I let my concerns for the day consume my time and attention, and I often find myself easily distracted and more readily occupied with things and people. Please forgive me. Right now, help me to put You first in my life and to reprioritize my responsibilities and other relationships around You. Thank You for helping me with this desire, Holy Spirit. In Christ Jesus's name. Amen.

Intercession

Pray for believers whose loyalties are divided between Christ and the world. Pray that they will make Christ their single focus.
🕊️ 🕊️ 🕊️

Dates:

Prayed _____ Answered _____

Personal Notes

_____

_____

_____

_____

_____

_____

_____

_____

_____

_____

_____

_____

_____

_____

_____

Dr. Marcia Livingston-Galloway

Community Concerns Multigenerational Prayers

Fellowshipping with Other Believers

And let us not neglect our meeting
together, as some people do, but encourage
one another, especially now that the
day of his return is drawing near.

—Hebrews 10:25 NLT

🙏 Prayer 🙏

Father God, thank You for the fellowship of believers. I often stay away from the community of believers when I am busy or feeling guilty about sin. In Your wisdom, You have provided the church community for us to fellowship and grow. So as we await the return of the Lord Jesus Christ, I commit to meeting with other believers regularly to find encouragement and to encourage others. Forgive me for the many times I have disobeyed this commandment, I pray. In Christ Jesus's name. Amen.

Intercession

Pray for Christian believers who have decided to isolate themselves from the fellowship of believers that God will help them realize that the enemy preys on sheep that do not stay with the fold.
🕊 🕊 🕊

Dates:

Prayed _____ Answered _____

Personal Notes

_____

_____

_____

_____

_____

_____

_____

_____

_____

_____

_____

_____

_____

_____

Dr. Marcia Livingston-Galloway

Humility in Worship

Come, let us worship and bow down. Let
us kneel before the LORD our maker,

—Psalm 95: 6 NLT

🙏 Prayer 🙏

Our heavenly Father, we glorify and thank You for access to Your presence. We enter Your throne room in awe and wonder of Your majesty! You are faithful, kind, just, merciful, gracious, forgiving, patient, caring, loving, thoughtful, encouraging, and consistent; and we are compelled to bow our heads, hearts, and knees before You. Father, we love and adore You. Father, thank You for coming to us in the form of Christ Jesus, Your Son. Holy Spirit, please help us this day and always to live lives of continual worship to the Most High God. In Christ Jesus's name. Amen.

Intercession

Ask God to open the eyes of the spiritually blind that they may see Jesus Christ in all His glory. 🕊 🕊 🕊

Dates:

Prayed _____ Answered _____

Personal Notes

_____

_____

_____

_____

_____

_____

_____

_____

_____

_____

_____

_____

_____

_____

_____

_____

_____

Interceding for Others

Then if my people who are called by my name
will humble themselves and pray and seek my
face and turn from their wicked ways, I will
hear from heaven and will forgive their sins and
restore their land. My eyes will be open and my
ears attentive to every prayer made in this place.

—2 Chronicles 7:14–15 NLT

🙏 Prayer 🙏

Dear heavenly Father, thank You for giving us Your name and making us part of Your family. We come before You today with honest hearts. We are sorry for sinning against You and our fellow men. We will not pretend we have it all together because we don't. We desperately need Your help to resist the devil and shun evil. We know You desire that we live like citizens of Your kingdom every day, and we want our lips to align with our lives. Lord, do not turn Your face away from us. We repent of our sins and turn from our wicked ways so our prayers may be heard and the people of all nations and the whole creation may be healed. In Christ Jesus's name. Amen.

Intercession

Pray for the leaders and members of your local church.
🕊 🕊 🕊

Dates:

Prayed _____ Answered _____

Personal Notes

_____

_____

_____

_____

_____

_____

_____

_____

_____

_____

_____

Praying Effectively
for Others

Confess your sins to each other and pray for
each other so that you may be healed. The
earnest prayer of a righteous person has great
power and produces wonderful results.

—James 5:16 NLT

🙏 Prayer 🙏

Eternal God and Father, thank You for the direct access that we have to Your throne room. We are incredibly grateful that we can come to You with our personal concerns and the concerns of others. Give us the boldness and humility to confess our faults and sins to others and to You and to pray for others that we, as the body of Christ, may be healed. We know only You can forgive sins, but we know that when we admit our sins to other humans, we also experience freedom and relief. Teach us how to pray earnestly like a horse at full gallop. Thank You for the community of believers. In Christ Jesus's name. Amen.

Intercession

Pray for your family, friends, and neighbors that they, too, may find freedom from sins through prayer and confession. 🕊️ 🕊️ 🕊️

Dates:

Prayed _____ Answered _____

Personal Notes

_____

_____

_____

_____

_____

_____

_____

_____

_____

_____

_____

_____

_____

_____

_____

_____

Forgiving Others

Instead, be kind to each other, tenderhearted,
forgiving one another, just as God
through Christ has forgiven you.

—Ephesians 4:32 NLT

🙏 Prayer 🙏

Great God and heavenly Father, thank You for Your genuine love and forgiveness toward me. You are the personification of compassion, patience, and kindness. I ask You to help me by the power of the Holy Spirit to forgive others just as Christ forgives and keeps forgiving me when I confess my sins. Please fill me with Your love, and help me to cooperate with the Holy Spirit as He seeks to cultivate Your qualities in me. Hallelujah! In Christ Jesus's name. Amen.

Intercession

Pray for people in all age groups who are suffering from emotional wounds, especially since childhood. Ask God to help them to forgive the perpetrators so they can begin to experience healing. 🕊️ 🕊️ 🕊️

Dates:

Prayed _____ Answered _____

Personal Notes

_____

_____

_____

_____

_____

_____

_____

_____

_____

_____

_____

_____

_____

_____

_____

Receiving Pardon for Guilt and Sin

Where is another God like you, who pardons
the guilt of the remnant, overlooking the
sins of his special people? You will not stay
angry with your people forever, because
you delight in showing unfailing love.

—Micah 7:18 NLT

Prayer

Father God, You are the God of patience, mercy, and forgiveness. Thank You for not staying angry with us when we disappoint and sin against You. We do not take You for granted. Help us to never allow our guilt to keep us away from You but to quickly seek Your forgiveness when we are wrong. Thank You for including us among Your special people and for the Holy Spirit who gives us the power to withstand temptation and to live a victorious Christian life. In Christ Jesus's name. Amen.

Intercession

Pray for those who are serving other gods and idols that the veil of darkness would be removed from their minds. 🕊 🕊 🕊

Dates:

Prayed _____ Answered _____

Personal Notes

_____

_____

_____

_____

_____

_____

_____

_____

_____

_____

_____

_____

_____

_____

Consideration for Others

Don't be selfish; don't try to impress others.
Be humble, thinking of others as better than
yourselves. Don't look out only for your own
interests, but take an interest in others, too.

—Philippians 2:3–4 NLT

🙏 Prayer 🙏

Father God who art in heaven, I come in Christ Jesus's name. Thank You, that You did not use Your equality with God to gain special favors. Instead, as an example, You humbled Yourself and became a lowly servant to serve hurting humanity. Thank You for showing us what true humility and love look like. Today, I ask You to help us to follow Your example. Show us what it means to put others' interests above our own, and teach us how to love genuinely and with humility and grace. In Christ Jesus's name. Amen.

Intercession

Pray for believers who turn others away from God and His kingdom because they are boastful, arrogant, and selfish. 🕊️ 🕊️ 🕊️

Dates:

Prayed _____ Answered _____

Personal Notes

_____

_____

_____

_____

_____

_____

_____

_____

_____

_____

_____

_____

_____

To Do What God Requires

No, O people, the Lord has told you what
is good, and this is what he requires of
you: to do what is right, to love mercy,
and to walk humbly with your God.

—Micah 6:8 NLT

🙏 Prayer 🙏

Father God, thank You for showing me what honors You. You care deeply about the people You've created, and You ask me to do the same. This week show me how to walk humbly alongside You, and as I do that, help me to act justly and mercifully. Show me how to reflect Your kind, loving, merciful presence to those around me. In Christ Jesus's name. Amen.

Intercession

Pray for believers across the globe that God's mercy, justice, and love would be depicted in our lives. 🕊 🕊 🕊

Dates:

Prayed _____ Answered _____

Personal Notes

_____

_____

_____

_____

_____

_____

_____

_____

_____

_____

_____

_____

_____

_____

_____

To Sow Good Seeds

Therefore, whenever we have the opportunity,
we should do good to everyone—especially
to those in the family of faith.

—Galatians 6:10 NLT

🙏 Prayer 🙏

Great God and Father, thank You for waking us up today to enjoy Your new mercies. So many times, we tend to selectively help others. We are guilty of looking out for only our families, friends, those who are close to us, and those who are easy to relate to. Please forgive us. Your word says to do good to everyone, especially to other believers. Please give us the grace to do good when You point out the opportunities. Help us to be the people who encourage, serve, and show compassion to others the way You serve and encourage us. In Christ Jesus's name. Amen.

Intercession

Pray for those in desperate need of help. Ask God to send someone their way today to bring relief and that they recognize it as God's response. 🕊 🕊 🕊

Dates:

Prayed _____ Answered _____

Personal Notes

_____

_____

_____

_____

_____

_____

_____

_____

_____

_____

_____

_____

_____

_____

To Cast Off the Spirit of Fear

For God has not given us a spirit of fear and timidity, but of power, love, and self-discipline.

—2 Timothy 1:7 NLT

🙏 Prayer 🙏

Great God and Father, Your name is Holy, and we trust in You. Thank You for giving us the spirit of power—the inner drive, ability, strength, and courage to be all You created us for. By Your spirit, we can forgive, love unconditionally, and serve others sincerely. Father, help us to practice self-discipline. Give us an awareness of Your abiding presence and protection, and renew our minds with Your truths. Thank You, Father. In Christ Jesus's name. Amen.

Intercession

Pray for people who are living in fear that they would encounter God's love and protection and develop disciplined minds. 🕊 🕊 🕊

Dates:

Prayed _____ Answered _____

Personal Notes

_____

_____

_____

_____

_____

_____

_____

_____

_____

_____

_____

_____

_____

_____

Trusting God for Protection

Those who trust in the Lord are as secure as
Mount Zion; they will not be defeated but
will endure forever. Just as the mountains
surround Jerusalem, so the Lord surrounds
his people, both now and forever.

—Psalm 125:1–2 NLT

🙏 Prayer 🙏

Merciful Father and Lord, thank You for keeping us and our families alive to see another day. We live in an unsafe and overcrowded environment, which has become more unsafe during this pandemic. We bring all our fears and anxieties to You and ask You to intervene. We know in our heads that we can overcome anything with You, but we need You to help us to believe it in our hearts. Your Word says that as the mountains are around Jerusalem, so You are around us forever. Thank You for this reassurance today. We renew our trust in You again and ask You to forgive us for living in fear. In Christ Jesus's name. Amen.

Intercession

Pray for the safety of those who live and work in fear-inducing environments. 🕊️ 🕊️ 🕊️

Dates:

Prayed _____ Answered _____

Personal Notes

_____

_____

_____

_____

_____

_____

_____

_____

_____

_____

_____

_____

_____

_____

_____

Dr. Marcia Livingston-Galloway

Finding Safety in God's Names

The name of the LORD is a strong fortress;
the godly run to him and are safe.

—Proverbs 18:10 NLT

🙏 Prayer 🙏

Great God and Father, I give You thanks, praise, and glory for today. I acknowledge You are Elohim (God), El Elyon (the Most High), El Shaddai (the Lord God Almighty), and Adonai (Master). When I am alone and afraid, please remind me that You are Jehovah Shammah (the Lord is There). If I'm tormented and troubled, You are Jehovah Shalom (the Lord is Peace) and Jehovah Ezer (the Lord My Help). Father, thank You that I can find safety in You every day and in every situation because You are the all-encompassing God! In Christ Jesus's name. Amen.

Intercession

Ask God to reveal other aspects of Himself to every believer as they read and meditate on His words. 🕊 🕊 🕊

Dates:

Prayed _____ Answered _____

Personal Notes

_____

_____

_____

_____

_____

_____

_____

_____

_____

_____

_____

_____

_____

_____

_____

Dr. Marcia Livingston-Galloway

Uplifting the Worried and Discouraged

Worry weighs a person down; an
encouraging word cheers a person up.

—Proverbs 12:25 NLT

🙏 Prayer 🙏

Dear Father God, thank You for giving me this day! I give You all the glory and praise for who You are and the peace You bring to my life. Help me to learn how to rest in Your presence. Although there are many different things happening in my immediate and extended family and in my personal life that are really causes for worry, help me not to be self-absorbed. In the midst of my own challenges, help me to be sensitive to those around me who are overwhelmed and worried about their challenges. Use me to bring joy, peace, and encouragement to someone else today; and teach me when to be silent. In Christ Jesus's name. Amen.

Intercession

Pray for parents and caregivers who are worrying about how they are going to provide for their families today. 🕊️ 🕊️ 🕊️

Dates:

Prayed_____ Answered_____

Personal Notes

_____

_____

_____

_____

_____

_____

_____

_____

_____

_____

_____

_____

_____

_____

_____

_____

Praying Instead of Worrying

Don't worry about anything; instead, pray
about everything. Tell God what you need,
and thank him for all he has done.

—Philippians 4:6 NLT

🙏 Prayer 🙏

Our God and eternal Father, today I awake with many concerns on my mind. Thank You for the many things You have done for me, my spouse, my family, my relatives, my friends, and my neighbors. I thank You in advance for supernatural uncommon favors with every person we will do business with (specify). Please give wisdom and direction to decision makers in every board room and courtroom today for the good of those who will be impacted by their decisions. Thank You for working behind the scenes. I give You thanks and praise. In Christ Jesus's name. Amen.

Intercession

Pray for those who are burdened by worry and sorrow that they would give them to Christ Jesus. 🕊️ 🕊️ 🕊️

Dates:

Prayed _____ Answered _____

Personal Notes

_____

_____

_____

_____

_____

_____

_____

_____

_____

_____

_____

_____

_____

_____

_____

_____

_____

Rescue from Trouble

The righteous person faces many troubles,
but the Lord comes to the rescue each time.

—Psalm 34:19 NLT

🙏 Prayer 🙏

Father God, it is a joy to be alive. Thank You for another day. We know the life of a Christian is not one without challenges. However, we know when we face trials, we do not have to face them alone because You are always there to rescue us from all of them or strengthen us to go through them. Thank You for caring about the things that trouble us and for Your commitment to always come to our aid. In Christ Jesus's name. Amen.

Intercession

Pray for those who have pending court cases that God's justice and judgment will prevail. 🕊️ 🕊️ 🕊️

Dates:

Prayed _____ Answered _____

Personal Notes

_____

_____

_____

_____

_____

_____

_____

_____

_____

_____

_____

_____

_____

_____

_____

Healing for the Sick

"LORD, help!" they cried in their trouble, and
he saved them from their distress. He sent
out his word and healed them, snatching
them from the door of death. Let them
praise the LORD for his great love and for the
wonderful things he has done for them.

—Psalm 107:19–21 NLT

🙏 Prayer 🙏

Most holy God and Father, thank You for being our Great
Physician. Today, we come to You with heavy hearts and ambiva-
lent faith. Our loved ones in the hospital are not doing well right
now. Many people have already lost loved ones suddenly because of
COVID-19 and other illnesses (name some), and there are those who
have been ill for a long time. We know You keep Your word and that
You care and are able to heal. Please guide the hands of all medical
personnel and caregivers and save our loved ones and all those who
are calling on You for healing and relief from their distress, especially
those who are yet to make Christ their Savior. Thank You for answer-
ing our prayers. In Christ Jesus's name. Amen.

Intercession

Pray earnestly for those grieving the deaths of their loved ones. Ask God to comfort their hearts. 🕊 🕊 🕊

Dates:

Prayed _____ Answered _____

Personal Notes

_____

_____

_____

_____

_____

_____

_____

_____

_____

_____

_____

_____

To Pray Effectively

"When you pray, don't babble on and
on as the Gentiles do. They think their
prayers are answered merely by repeating
their words again and again. Don't be like
them, for your Father knows exactly what
you need even before you ask him!

—Matthew 6:7–8 NLT

🙏 Prayer 🙏

Great God and Father, thank You for the privilege of a new day and for allowing me to have honest conversations with You. I ask Your forgiveness for praying to You with wrong and selfish motives. Help me to put away arrogance and pride and to come to you with honesty, sincerity, and humility. Help me to be specific in my prayers and to call my sins by the same names you give to them instead of glossing over them. In Christ Jesus's name. Amen.

Intercession

Pray for those who struggle to pray to God. Ask God to teach them how to converse with Him! 🕊 🕊 🕊

Dates:

Prayed _____ Answered _____

Personal Notes

_____

_____

_____

_____

_____

_____

_____

_____

_____

_____

_____

_____

_____

_____

To Persist in Prayer

"Keep on asking, and you will receive what you ask for. Keep on seeking, and you will find. Keep on knocking, and the door will be opened to you. For everyone who asks, receives. Everyone who seeks, finds. And to everyone who knocks, the door will be opened.

—Matthew 7:7–8 NLT

🙏 Prayer 🙏

Gracious Father God, thank You for the open access I have to You all day, every day. Lord, I have the tendency to give up quickly when I do not see the answers I am expecting and in the timeline that I set. Help me to be patient and not to give up so easily but to keep on praying until I see Your answer. Open my eyes that I may see the answers when You send them. When I am about to give up, remind me that You mean it when You say You hear my prayers and will answer them all. In Christ Jesus's name. Amen.

Intercession

Pray for those who have been praying about a situation and are about to give up because they have not seen the answer they are expecting. 🕊 🕊 🕊

Dates:

Prayed _____ Answered _____

Personal Notes

_____

_____

_____

_____

_____

_____

_____

_____

_____

_____

_____

_____

_____

_____

Knowing the Father's Love

The Lord is like a father to his children, tender
and compassionate to those who fear him.

—Psalm 103:13 NLT

🙏 Prayer 🙏

Heavenly Father, thank You for all You have already done for us. If You never did one more thing for us, we would still give you thanks. Even when our pain and suffering are a result of our willful disobedience, You always show compassion toward us. We experience Your mercy and grace every day and appreciate that You do not treat us as we truly deserve. Please continue to work in us in spite of our failures, and help us to develop a holy fear and reverence for You. Help us to practice compassion and patience with others as You do with us. In Christ Jesus's name. Amen.

Intercession

Pray for fathers and for children who are being raised without a father figure in their lives. 🕊️ 🕊️ 🕊️

Dates:

Prayed _____ Answered _____

Personal Notes

_____

_____

_____

_____

_____

_____

_____

_____

_____

_____

_____

_____

_____

_____

Casting All Cares on God

Give all your worries and cares to
God, for he cares about you.

—1 Peter 5:7 NLT

🙏 Prayer 🙏

Our Father in heaven, I bow my heart before You today in holy reverence. Thank You for being my life source, refuge, protector, and strength. When I am troubled, tempted, or faced with trials, cause me to remember that You care and are waiting to take my burdens when I give them to You. So today, Lord, here are my burdens. I ask You to take them. Thank You for listening and caring for me. In Christ Jesus's name. Amen.

Intercession

Pray for believers and people everywhere who are burdened with sin, worries, and cares that they would give them to God and not take them from Him again. 🕊️ 🕊️ 🕊️

Dates:

Prayed _____ Answered _____

Personal Notes

_____

_____

_____

_____

_____

_____

_____

_____

_____

_____

_____

_____

_____

_____

_____

To Practice Wisdom in Ministry

"Look, I am sending you out as sheep
among wolves. So be as shrewd as
snakes and harmless as doves.

—Matthew 10:16 NLT

🙏 Prayer 🙏

Gracious, loving, and eternal Father, thank You for waking us up this morning and clothing us in our right minds. We know every person we meet does not always have good intentions toward us, and that there are people who take pleasure in mistreating us and others, especially because we serve You. Thank You for being there when this happens. Help us to respond to people and things in a way that is wise and harmless. We pray You will give us peace, strength, and wisdom to manage all situations. In Christ Jesus's name. Amen.

Intercession

Pray for people who are quick-tempered and who react to things quickly and unwisely instead of prayerfully. 🕊 🕊 🕊

Dates:

Prayed _____ Answered _____

Personal Notes

_____

_____

_____

_____

_____

_____

_____

_____

_____

_____

_____

_____

_____

_____

Dr. Marcia Livingston-Galloway

For Discernment

From the tribe of Issachar, there were 200
leaders of the tribe with their relatives. All
these men understood the signs of the times
and knew the best course for Israel to take.

—1 Chronicles 12:32 NLT

🙏 Prayer 🙏

Everlasting Father and Lord, thank You for the privilege of having free access to You every day. Right now, there are many moving parts in our lives and several decisions that we need to make. Please give us Your wisdom, insight, and guidance. You are the God of times and seasons, and we want to be in synchrony with You. Like the sons of Issachar, help us to accurately discern the time. Show us what we should be doing in these times, and instruct us on how to proceed in every matter. Thank You for Your help and guidance and good success. In Christ Jesus's name. Amen.

Intercession

Pray for leaders and decision makers at all levels across the nations that God would give them discernment and direction today.
🕊️ 🕊️ 🕊️

Dates:

Prayed_____ Answered_____

Personal Notes

_____

_____

_____

_____

_____

_____

_____

_____

_____

_____

_____

_____

_____

_____

_____

_____

To Love Sincerely

Dear friends, let us continue to love one
another, for love comes from God. Anyone
who loves is a child of God and knows
God. But anyone who does not love
does not know God, for God is love.

—1 John 4:7–8 NLT

🙏 Prayer 🙏

Father God, thank You for permission to enter Your throne room every day. Thank you for Your compassion and unconditional love. Today we ask You to teach us how to love sincerely from the heart. You love us in spite of all our mess and shortcomings. Give us the grace and patience we need to show genuine love to every person we come in contact with. Father, because of our relationship to You and with You, we are able to love our fellow men. Thank You for Your grace. In Christ Jesus's name. Amen.

Intercession

Pray for the wicked, especially those who nurture hatred in their hearts. 🕊 🕊 🕊

Dates:

Prayed _____ Answered _____

Personal Notes

_____

_____

_____

_____

_____

_____

_____

_____

_____

_____

_____

_____

_____

_____

_____

To Know and Follow God's Instructions

The instructions of the Lord are perfect,
reviving the soul. The decrees of the Lord
are trustworthy, making wise the simple.

—Psalm 19:7 NLT

🙏 Prayer 🙏

Dear Father God, thank You for Your living word and the instructions it entails for every aspect of human life. It is Your word that has revived our souls and has provided the instructions we need for godliness. Your word is trustworthy and is not as complicated as we make it to be. Today we ask You to put an unsatisfying desire in us for Your word. As we read the Bible, help us to understand it and resolve to consistently obey Your decrees that You have written in it. Holy Father, we are grateful for Jesus Christ who lived by Your word and obeyed it even when He faced death. We praise you for renewing our minds. In Christ Jesus's name. Amen.

Intercession

Pray for believers everywhere. Ask God to help them to develop an appetite and hunger for His word and an obedient heart. 🕊 🕊 🕊

Dates:

Prayed _____ Answered _____

Personal Notes

_____

_____

_____

_____

_____

_____

_____

_____

_____

_____

To Forgive Offenses

Make allowance for each other's faults, and
forgive anyone who offends you. Remember, the
Lord forgave you, so you must forgive others.

—Colossians 3:13 NLT

🙏 Prayer 🙏

Holy Father and Lord, thank You for Your forgiveness. Since
You have forgiven us of our many sins, we can forgive others. We
confess that letting go of hurtful circumstances and forgiving others
is not an easy task. So please help us to be more like You and help
us to forgive those who have hurt us quickly. Rid us of all bitterness,
anger, and offense. In Christ Jesus's name. Amen.

Intercession

Pray for those who are quick to find faults in others and who
practice self-righteousness. Ask God to give them a humble heart.
🕊️ 🕊️ 🕊️

Dates:

Prayed _____ Answered _____

Personal Notes

_____

_____

_____

_____

_____

_____

_____

_____

_____

_____

_____

_____

_____

_____

To Live in Harmony
with Others

May God, who gives this patience
and encouragement, help you live in
complete harmony with each other, as is
fitting for followers of Christ Jesus.

—Romans 15:5 NLT

🙏 Prayer 🙏

Gracious Father God, thank You for inviting us into Your family. We admit we are impatient with people and find it difficult to work with those who are very different from us. We are often in disagreement with other believers and contribute to the disharmony in the group. Father, we do not want to be like that, so we ask for your forgiveness and help today. In Christ Jesus's name. Amen.

Intercession

Pray for immature believers who cause division in the body of Christ and those who are uncooperative. 🕊️ 🕊️ 🕊️

Dates:

Prayed _____ Answered _____

Personal Notes

_____

_____

_____

_____

_____

_____

_____

_____

_____

_____

_____

_____

_____

_____

_____

_____

Patience and Hope
in Times of Trouble

Rejoice in our confident hope. Be patient
in trouble, and keep on praying.

—Romans 12:12 NLT

🙏 Prayer 🙏

Father God, we thank You for Your word because it brings great encouragement and joy even in our moments of fear and distress. Right now, we are in a difficult season in our lives, in our nation, and in our world. It seems like things and people are reeling out of control. Yet Your word reminds us today that even now, we do not have to give in to hopelessness. Give us peace even when we are unsure how things will turn out. Help us to stay in prayer during seasons of trouble and struggles. We put our hope in You. In Christ Jesus's name. Amen.

Intercession

Pray for children and adults who are experiencing emotional pain, financial struggles, and relationship challenges that they will find hope and peace in God. 🕊 🕊 🕊

Dates:

Prayed _____ Answered _____

Personal Notes

_____

_____

_____

_____

_____

_____

_____

_____

_____

_____

_____

_____

_____

_____

Deliverance from Evil

And don't let us yield to temptation,
but rescue us from the evil one.

—Matthew 6:13 NLT

🙏 Prayer 🙏

Heavenly Father, we thank You for today and Your many blessings and mercy. Thank You for defeating the devil at Calvary and making us more than conquerors. Help us not to yield to the temptations to sin, and help us to resist the devil and to identify the ways of escape that You show us. Thank You, Father. In Christ Jesus's name. Amen.

Intercession

Pray for others whom you know who need to be delivered from the bondage of sin. 🕊️ 🕊️ 🕊️

Dates:

Prayed _____ Answered _____

Personal Notes

_____

_____

_____

_____

_____

_____

_____

_____

_____

_____

_____

_____

_____

Dr. Marcia Livingston-Galloway

Overcoming Evil with Good

Don't let evil conquer you, but
conquer evil by doing good.

—Romans 12:21 NLT

🙏 Prayer 🙏

Gracious Father God, thank You for the access we have to You because of Jesus's finished work on Calvary's cross. Thank You for showing us kindness even when we don't deserve it. We know our natural response is to hurt and retaliate against those who do us wrong. Cleanse our hearts and minds of every evil thought and motive, and help us to show Your kindness and love to those who offend or hurt us. We want to be an example of Christ to all who we interact with. In Christ Jesus's name. Amen.

Intercession

Pray today for people who thrive on doing evil and for God's protection for those who are in danger. 🕊 🕊 🕊

Dates:

Prayed _____ Answered _____

Personal Notes

_____

_____

_____

_____

_____

_____

_____

_____

_____

_____

_____

_____

_____

_____

_____

Trusting God to Work on My Behalf

And we know that God causes everything
to work together for the good of
those who love God and are called
according to his purpose for them.

—Romans 8:28 NLT

🙏 Prayer 🙏

Gracious Father God, today I pause to say thank You for being active in my life. I know You are aware of everything that affects me, the good and the bad. I don't know how the troubles (specify what your concerns are) I am facing will work out, but I believe You are working things out behind the scenes. Father, help my faith, and help me to put away fear and anxiety. You have helped me before, and I am grateful. The situation does not look good or feel good, but You are working it out for my good and Your glory. Let it be so, I pray in the name of Christ Jesus. Amen.

Intercession

Pray for someone who is in deep trouble that they will turn to God. 🕊 🕊 🕊

Dates:

Prayed _____ Answered _____

Personal Notes

_____

_____

_____

_____

_____

_____

_____

_____

_____

_____

_____

_____

_____

_____

Dr. Marcia Livingston-Galloway

Safety and Security in God

My God is my rock, in whom I find protection.
He is my shield, the power that saves me,
and my place of safety. He is my refuge, my
savior, the one who saves me from violence.

—2 Samuel 22:3 NLT

🙏 Prayer 🙏

My Gracious Father, Savior, and Lord, thank You for Your protection. We know sometimes we put more confidence in man-made protection like alarm systems, law enforcement officers, and even other people. Thank You for the assurance that the enemy cannot defeat us because You are our Rock, Security, Protection, Hiding Place, and Defense. Therefore, we are not anxious, fearful, or worried. Hallelujah! We are safe! In Christ Jesus's name. Amen.

Intercession

Pray for the young and elderly who are homeless and subject to harm in your country and across the globe. 🕊️ 🕊️ 🕊️

Dates:

Prayed _____ Answered _____

Personal Notes

_____

_____

_____

_____

_____

_____

_____

_____

_____

_____

_____

_____

_____

_____

_____

To Experience God's Rest

He lets me rest in green meadows; he leads
me beside peaceful streams. He renews
my strength. He guides me along right
paths, bringing honor to his name.

—Psalm 23:2–3 NLT

🙏 Prayer 🙏

Father God, thank You for being our Good Shepherd who continues to watch over us. We are concerned about our safety, although we know that with You, we are safe and protected. Like sheep, we often wander off from You and end up in danger. Please help us to keep our eyes on You and to follow Your leading each day. Thank You for the assurance that You will never leave us in danger. We trust Your leadership and appreciate the pleasant places You provide for our rest and restoration. Thank You for your loving care. In Christ Jesus's name. Amen.

Intercession

Pray for ministers of the gospel who are physically, mentally, and emotionally fatigued that God will help them to make time for rest, restoration, and relaxation. 🕊️ 🕊️ 🕊️

Dates:

Prayed _____ Answered _____

Personal Notes

_____

_____

_____

_____

_____

_____

_____

_____

_____

_____

_____

_____

_____

_____

_____

To Keep God's Commandments

Those who accept my commandments
and obey them are the ones who love me.
And because they love me, my Father
will love them. And I will love them
and reveal myself to each of them."

—John 14:21 NLT

🙏 Prayer 🙏

Great Father God, thank You for loving us unconditionally. You have called us into a love relationship with You. Help us to demonstrate our love for You by obeying all Your commandments. We are prone to disobedience, selfishness, and self-obsession and have the tendency to question Your instructions at times. Please forgive us, and help us to remember that none of Your commandments is burdensome. In Christ Jesus's name. Amen.

Intercession

Pray for all believers that we might demonstrate our love for God by keeping His commandments. 🕊 🕊 🕊

Dates:

Prayed _____ Answered _____

Personal Notes

_____

_____

_____

_____

_____

_____

_____

_____

_____

_____

_____

_____

_____

_____

_____

To Live as Kingdom Citizens

For he has rescued us from the kingdom
of darkness and transferred us into
the Kingdom of his dear Son,

—Colossians 1:13 NLT

🙏 Prayer 🙏

Father God, thank You for rescuing us from darkness and evil and registering our names in Your kingdom registry. Thank You for loving us so much that You would wrestle with the devil for us. Now that You have delivered us from darkness, we can walk in the light of Jesus Christ, Your Son. We are excited that we have a new home in Your kingdom. Help us to live like free citizens in Your kingdom and to remember that the enemy no longer has a hold on our lives. We are free, and we are safe. Praise the Lord! Hallelujah! In Christ Jesus's name. Amen.

Intercession

Pray for those who are still trapped in the kingdom of darkness that they will see and accept God's offer of deliverance. 🕊️ 🕊️ 🕊️

Dates:

Prayed _____ Answered _____

Personal Notes

_____

_____

_____

_____

_____

_____

_____

_____

_____

_____

_____

_____

_____

_____

_____

_____

_____

Forgiveness For All

You forgave the guilt of your people—
yes, you covered all their sins.

—Psalm 85:2 NLT

🙏 Prayer 🙏

Gracious Father God, thank You for demonstrating your love for Your people by sending Jesus Christ to die for all of us. Each day we awake, we experience Your grace and mercy even though we don't deserve it. You always take the first step toward us even when we remain stubborn and rebellious. Every day You extend Your hand of forgiveness, and today we extend our hands in surrender and acceptance. We are grateful that Jesus did not die for some of our sins but all: past, present, and future. We are forever indebted and grateful to You. Thank You for Your patience and endless love. In Christ Jesus's name. Amen.

Intercession

Pray for the unsaved, especially those who are guilt-ridden and find it difficult to embrace God's forgiveness. 🕊️ 🕊️ 🕊️

Dates:

Prayed _____ Answered _____

Personal Notes

_____

_____

_____

_____

_____

_____

_____

_____

_____

_____

_____

_____

_____

_____

_____

_____

Jabez Benediction

He was the one who prayed to the God of
Israel, "Oh, that you would bless me and
expand my territory! Please be with me in all
that I do, and keep me from all trouble and
pain!" And God granted him his request.

—1 Chronicles 4:10 NLT

🙏 Prayer 🙏

Father God, thank you for giving life to me. As I travel along
life's journey, I ask that You bless me in every work of my hands and
expand my territory and my spheres of influence. Thank You for
Your abiding presence and Your protection from trouble and pain. I
rest in You. In Christ Jesus's name. Amen.

Intercession

Pray the above prayer over your family, other believers, and
those whom God places in your sphere of influence. Call the names
of those you know. 🕊 🕊 🕊

Dates:

Prayed _____ Answered _____

Personal Notes

_____

_____

_____

_____

_____

_____

_____

_____

_____

_____

_____

_____

_____

_____

_____

_____

Generational Benediction

May the Lord bless you and protect
you. May the Lord smile on you and
be gracious to you. May the Lord show
you his favor and give you his peace.

—Numbers 6:24–26 NLT

🙏 Prayer 🙏

Heavenly Father, I give You thanks for blessing me and protecting me. I ask You to continue to smile on me and to be gracious to me. I anticipate and embrace Your favor and peace on this day. In Christ Jesus's name. Amen.

Intercession

Pray the above prayer over your family, other believers, and those who God places in your sphere of influence. Call the names of those you know. 🕊 🕊 🕊

Dates:

Prayed _____ Answered _____

Personal Notes

_____

_____

_____

_____

_____

_____

_____

_____

_____

_____

_____

_____

_____

_____

A Farewell Benediction

In times of trouble, may the LORD answer your
cry. May the name of the God of Jacob keep
you safe from all harm. May he send you help
from his sanctuary and strengthen you from
Jerusalem. May he remember all your gifts and
look favorably on your burnt offerings. *Interlude*
May he grant your heart's desires and make
all your plans succeed. May we shout for
joy when we hear of your victory and raise
a victory banner in the name of our God.
May the Lord answer all your prayers.

—Psalm 20:1–5 NLT

🙏 Prayer 🙏

Most righteous God and eternal Father, I am forever grateful
for the assurance that in times of trouble, You will hear and answer
my cries. Thank You for keeping me safe from all harm, sending me
help every time I need it, and strengthening me in my times of weak-
ness. I know that every gift that I have comes from You, so I humbly
offer them back to You in worship. Please grant me the desires of my
heart that please You and give me good success in everything I set
my hands to do. I believe that my Christian brothers and sisters will
rejoice with me when my plans succeed and I am victorious over the

enemy. I am confident that You still hear and answer all my prayers. In Christ Jesus's name. Amen.

Intercession

Pray the above prayer, inserting the names of your family, other believers, and those who God places in your sphere of influence.

Dates:

Prayed _____ Answered _____

Personal Notes

_____

_____

_____

_____

_____

_____

_____

_____

_____

_____

About the Author

Dr. Marcia Livingston-Galloway is an inspiring, knowledgeable, and exceptional faith-based educational leader, mentor, and consultant. She is highly respected and known for the unique, creative, engaging, and cutting-edge teaching strategies she employs when conducting a Bible study or any academic learning activity. Her passion is fueled by an unwavering belief that believers who regularly engage in sincere prayer and Bible study will experience an intimate transformative relationship with God that will empower them to integrate their faith in every aspect of their lives.

Dr. Livingston-Galloway is a lifelong learner who immerses herself in the most relevant and up-to-date research and practices in the field of education so she is able to adapt quickly to the ever-changing learning landscape. She is the founder of The Teacher Consultants and serves as an adjunct senior professor at Oral Roberts University in Tulsa, Oklahoma.

Her exceptional communication skills, dedication to relationship building, and ability to effortlessly connect with individuals across cultures have made her a sought-after keynote speaker and presenter at numerous Christian and academic conferences, seminars, convocations, and panel discussions locally and internationally.

Dr. Livingston-Galloway is an ordained minister and a member of the ministerial staff at Revelations Revealed Truth Evangelistic Center (RRTEC), Tulsa, Oklahoma, with oversight over the Prayer and Intercessory Ministry. She is married to Milton M. Galloway and resides in Port St. Lucie, Florida.

Printed in the USA
CPSIA information can be obtained
at www.ICGtesting.com
CBHW021340051223
2288CB00015BA/12